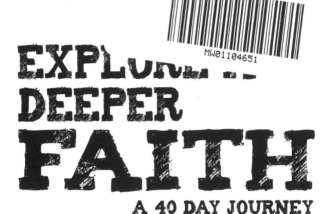

EXPLORING A
DEEPER
FAITH

A 40 DAY JOURNEY

BRAD GUEST

DEDICATION

To my children, because of your energy and love, it drives me to become a better man, husband, father, pastor, and most importantly, follower of Christ.

DAY 1
STATUS QUO

Several years ago I told a group of church people to look around the room and tell me what the church would look like in 25 years if it did not change. The group of people gathered were older and seemed to understand the ramifications of just gathering with the same people without any new growth. The church was going to die.

I later overheard one of the men from that meeting in a back hallway with a deacon berating my comments and basically saying that we needed to just keep on with the status quo.

The natural inclination of all of us is to get nice and cozy in our comfort zones. We hunker down with a group of people, in a particular place, or in a particular church and just get comfortable.

We have a great calling to not just settle for the status quo but to push forward into areas that seem uncertain. Faith demands that we do so. In Jim Putman's *real-life discipleship training manual* he says, "The church was not designed to be a group of spectators who attend weekly lectures; it was designed to be a trained army with a powerful message."

Romans 10:14 says, "How, then, can they call on the one they have not believed in? And how can they believe in the one of whom they have not heard? And how can they hear without someone preaching to them?" If we are settling for the status quo, these questions will be left unanswered.

NOAHism
LEARNING NEW CULTURE

"What language do they speak
in Spokane?"

DAY 2
REFRESHED

In Matthew 26, Jesus caps the section on Judas' betrayal kiss with "then all the disciples' deserted Him and ran away (v56)." What a sad sentence to describe a group of men who Jesus had poured into for over three years. They felt the pressure of persecution and fled.

When pondering on this verse, I quickly realize that the tragedy is not the disciples deserted Jesus, but that I do the same with no persecution. I do it through wasting time, poor money decisions, and by not fully using my gifts to multiply His kingdom.

Acts 3:19 tells me that I need to "repent, then, and turn to God, so that your sins may be wiped out, that times of refreshing may come from the Lord." Repentance is not a popular word these days. We don't like to admit we are wrong or turn around and go another direction dictated by someone else. But if we are going to have a life that means more than just chasing after the elusive American Dream, we must turn to God so that we can be refreshed, live a life of purpose, and be in step with Jesus, not kicking up dust in the opposite direction.

NOAHism
MAX LUCADO'S GREATEST
ACHIEVEMENT

"Hey, that's the guy from the bug movie (Hermie)!"

DAY 3
EQUIPPED?

One of my favorite authors passed away in 2012, Ray Bradbury. In *Fahrenheit 451* there is a great quote: "You don't have to burn books to destroy a culture. Just get people to stop reading them."

As I thought on this quote and thought about society, I was burdened by our lack of depth. We have, seemingly overnight, become a "text" society, instead of a pick up a book and grow mentally, physically, and most importantly spiritually society.

I read stories of people all over the world gathering in small, dimly lit rooms to hear a few pages of the Bible that have been smuggled in read to them. They do this under severe persecution that could mean prison, beating, or death.

We gather around an iPhone to see the latest Facebook status or to read the latest sentence fragment from a text. Why don't we feed on the Word and allow it to grow us into the spiritually mature disciples of Christ that we are supposed to be?

2 Timothy 3:16 says, "All Scripture is God-breathed and is useful for teaching, rebuking, correcting and training in righteousness, so that the servant of God may be thoroughly equipped for every good work."

I sometimes think that Satan does not have to bring out the big weapons of mass destruction on us because we are becoming more and more isolated the more and more we become connected electronically and the less time the Bible actually spends soaking into our hearts.

We are equipped in this modern technological world, but equipped for what?

NOAHism
MAKING TIME COUNT

Noah: I'm so mad at you I'm not going to look at you for 100 minutes.

Nia: That's only 2 hours!

Noah: Ok, 100 hours then!

Nia: That's more like it!

DAY 4
PATHWAYS

Jeremiah 29:11 says, "For I know the plans I have for you- [this is] the Lord's declaration- "plans for [your] welfare, not for disaster, to give you a future and a hope."

I got the opportunity to share at church a little about a chapter in our lives that was very difficult and the result after going through this time. What I realize now in the quiet of the moment is that clarity is hard to grasp in the midst of troubling times. When disease or death strikes. When marriage is difficult. When life crashes in fast and furious.

If we pause for a moment and take a firm grasp of the promise of Jeremiah 29:11, we can find peace and clarity in the promise that this storm did not catch God by surprise. He only allows it for growth (for welfare) and in its end, gives us a future and a hope.

The Scripture goes on to say in v12-13, "You will call to Me and come and pray to Me, and I will listen to you.

You will seek Me and find me when you search for Me with all your heart." We are never alone on our pathway. God is watching and He is listening in our moments of grief and tragedy, pain and sorrow, and in our times of peace and prosperity.

Whatever pathway you find yourself on during life's journey, cry out to Him as Psalm 46:1 says, "God is our refuge and strength, a helper who is always found in times of trouble."

MODERNIZED ORDINANCE

Noah has served us The Lord's Supper twice today with broken pancakes and tap water (just like Jesus did many years ago).

DAY 5
COMMUNITY

I've always been told that life takes off at a rapid pace after graduating high school. This statement must be true because I feel like I graduated yesterday and it has been far too many years ago to mention. I also remember being a young preacher and the men who poured into me. They took time out of their busy schedules to share a word of wisdom or to meet me for a coffee and talk about whatever it was I was struggling with at the time.

When you read through the Gospels, pay attention to how Jesus used His time to minister to others. You will see that there are times when He spoke to crowds, to smaller groups of peoples, to the twelve disciples, to an inner circle of three disciples, and times when He spoke one on one with people.

Hebrews 10:24-25 says, "And let us be concerned about one another in order to promote love and good works, not staying away from our meetings, as some habitually do, but encouraging each another, and all the more as you see the day drawing near." Too many times what we promote in our relationships with people is not love or good works, but gossip and slander.

We are created to live in community. We are created to use our gifts, experiences, hurts, and hardships to encourage each other. How are you doing at building these types of relationships?

NOAHism
GOD'S DESIGN

Beth: Noah, you've got to stop licking your lips!

Noah: They are not going to fall off. They are stuck on your head really tight!

DAY 6
EXERCISE

The day seems to slip away with me laying in bed looking at the ceiling and saying, "I need to exercise." Spending time with God leads to getting the kids breakfast which leads to dishes which leads to laundry and then the day begins and before I know it it's bed time.

In the midst of all the stressors that surround each of our lives we must find an outlet, to not only keep our bodies healthy, but to keep our minds and spirits in tune. I got to take a few minutes tonight, as my wife pushed me out of the door to go for a run. Even though I was gone all of ten minutes, I returned knowing exactly this is what has been missing in my life to bring balance.

1 Timothy 4:8 says, "the training of the body has a limited benefit, but godliness is beneficial in every way, since it holds promise for the present life and also for the life to come." I've heard this verse so many times explained from the "let's be focused on being godly because it has the most benefit" side. The limited side of

this verse is rarely explained.

It is true that exercise can become an idol and we worship the idea of the way we look and how others look at us. It is also true that some people neglect exercise to the detriment of their health, and thus, their effectiveness for the kingdom of God is limited.

Just maybe exercise, in its "limited benefit," is just enough to sharpen our minds, calm our spirits, and keep us going one more step to impact the kingdom of God to our fullest.

NOAHism
SUPERHERO ATTRACTION

While looking at his Batman DS game, Noah asks, "Why are Catwoman's lips so juicy?"

DAY 7
COMMUNICATION

Imagine for a moment driving on a highway with no directional or speed limit signs. If you live in Mississippi, you may not need to imagine. What kind of chaos would ensue? Imagine if there were no stop signs or stop lights. People could have the right heart and try to create an order, but what about the majority? Would they know to follow the same unwritten order?

Communication is vital when it comes to any relationship. In marriages, besides finances, I would say (no scientific proof) that this is the biggest downfall of the bond of marriage. One or the other either does not communicate well or at all. On teams, whether they be athletic, church, or in business, the breakdown comes when directives are ordered without reasoning communicated or when different factions go renegade and do their on things without regard to the organization.

Healthy relationships are built on a lot of things, but a big component is communication. Proverbs 13:17 says,

"A wicked messenger falls into trouble, but a trustworthy courier brings healing."

The challenge for each of us to examine how we communicate with our spouses, children, coworkers, and people in general. When we notice the areas where we are "a wicked messenger," we must be willing to repent and change the behavior.

How are you communicating?

NOAHism
POP CULTURE

Listening to a song by Taylor Swift, Noah says, "Nia, you know that is Justin Beaver singing. He sings like a girl, ya know?"

DAY 8
MOTIVATION

Mark 3 is filled with people who wanted a piece of Jesus' time. On the surface you might think that we should seek Jesus, to strive to be with Him whenever we can, but this very diverse group of people had very selfish, different motivation.

The religious elite sought to be in Jesus' presence to see if He would do something against their law "in order to accuse Him (v2)" and them plot against Him (v6). The "great multitude followed...because they heard about everything He was doing (v7-8)." The disciples were unlearned and in constant need of His teaching (v13-15). His family wanted "to restrain Him because...He's out of His mind (v21)."

What is my motivation for seeking Jesus? What drives my devotion to Christ? Am I chasing hard after what He will give or what He will heal in my life? Or am I desperately chasing without abandon for who He is, the Son of God?

God demands obedience. This obedience should be displayed in our chase after Him with reckless abandon, no matter what the circumstances are in our lives.

To truly be a disciple of Christ we must be able to answer the following questions:

- If He doesn't heal me or my loved one, will I still trust and obey Him?
- If He doesn't allow me to have children or a spouse, will I still love and follow Him?
- If I never receive admiration or praise in my job, family, or in recreation, will I honor and praise Him?
- If I see little fruit for my labors, will I persevere and seek strength in my relationship with Him?

What is my motivation in my devotion to Christ?

NOAHism
1ST DAY OF SCHOOL

Me: Did you make any friends today?

Noah: I asked one boy to be my friend and he said not yet!

DAY 9
OBEDIENCE

PARENT: Clean your room!

CHILD: Why do I have to?

PARENT: Because I told you to!

Sound familiar? I have noticed in my parenting expertise that I often fall back to the standard "because I told you to" lazy parenting. Not only that, if you take time to listen in on the wave of today's culture, this lazy approach is taking root in every area of society.

This is one of the reasons I love Scripture. We are instructed to be obedient and then given the context for the obedience. Let me challenge you with three areas.

After we start a relationship with Christ, the first act of obedience Jesus gives new believers is to be baptized. Baptism does not save you, but tells the world where your identity is held. It is a symbolic, public testimony of dying to your sinful self, burying the dead person, and being raised to new life in Christ. I challenge you to talk with a trusted friend about being baptized if you have never taken this first step of obedience.

Second, participating in the Lord's Supper. I remember vividly when I was growing up how somber and tradionalized the ordinance was. No smiling, no looking at your neighbor. Take the stale, square of bread and the grape juice and be quiet. The Lord's Supper is an act of obedience of how we identify and are connected to Christ and the church. It signifies the broken body of Christ and spilt blood of Jesus Christ. The Lord's Supper is an important time of reflection about our actions and our faith, a remembrance of what was accomplished on the cross, and also a renewal of our love for each other. (2 Corinthians 9:6-8)

Third, giving generously to the cause of Christ. I am not going to give an arbitrary percentage to strive for. Just remember that all we have belongs to God anyways. Only through His gifting of us, His protection of us, and His guidance of us are we able to earn anything in our lives. I challenge you to check your bank statement, clarify what are needs and what are wants, and pray about what you can change about your spending habits. Give first, spend later. God promises to "make every grace overflow" so that we will have "everything we need." (2 Corinthians 9:6-8)

- If you've never been baptized, talk to a friend about taking this step.
- Start viewing the Lord Supper in light of Scripture and in understanding of what it personally means to you.
- Begin this month giving a percentage of your income to a local church to further the work of the kingdom of Christ.

34

NOAHism
NINJA FRIENDS

"We would be playing on the playground then he would get away from me and I couldn't find him!"

DAY 10
JUGGLING

I'm not any good at juggling. I've acquired the ability to juggle two objects in one hand, with some consistency, but when I try three in two hands, I cannot make it around one time. I always end of catching one and letting the other two fall to the ground. What I know is that I spend too much time focused on one object and disregard the other two. This causes me to get way too involved on one thing and cause failure on the other two.

Life is just like this. We must acquire the ability to learn from yesterday, live in today, and plan for tomorrow. If we get too focused on any on the three and disregard the other two, we end up causing failure to everything.

Life is not meant to be spent enslaved on mistakes we made in the past. We must learn from those mistakes and understand that when we are forgiven, we are never unforgiven for that action. 1 John 1:9 says, "If we confess our sins, He is faithful and righteous to forgive us our sins and to cleanse us from all unrighteousness." It is outside of the character of God to cast your failure back in your face. If you are uncertain of this fact, search the Scriptures and see for yourself.

We must plan for tomorrow. God's grace is sufficient. His providence is out in front of us. I believe these statements wholeheartedly. We are still required to prepare ourselves for what God is going to bless us with. The best example I can think of is of John the Baptist. In Mark 1, we read, "The beginning of the gospel of Jesus Christ, the Son of God. As it is written in Isaiah the prophet: Look, I am sending My messenger ahead of You, who will prepare Your way. A voice of one crying out in the wilderness: Prepare the way for the Lord; make His paths straight! John came baptizing in the wilderness and preaching a baptism of repentance for the forgiveness of sins."

Think for a moment if Isaiah would not have presented this message. Think for a moment if John the Baptist would not have stepped in and prepared the way for Jesus to come. I'm not intelligent enough to presume what the outcome would be. The coming of Jesus took much preparation, it took obedient servants, and it took tremendous foresight of what was to come.

Are we living in so much of a different time? What are we preparing for? The return of Christ. We are building His kingdom. We must be prepared for the harvest that God is going to give us. What if God gives us 2,000 souls tomorrow? How will we disciple them? How will we make sure they become fully devoted followers of Christ?

As we learn from yesterday and plan for tomorrow, we must execute today. Today is the only time we have to put to practice what we have learned and carry out the plans that have been prepared. 2 Corinthians 6:2 says, "Today is the day of salvation!"

James puts it this way in chapter 1, "But be doers of the word and not hearers only, deceiving yourselves. Because if anyone is a hearer of the word and not a doer, he is like a man looking at his own face in a mirror. For he looks at himself, goes away, and immediately forgets what kind of man he was. But the one who looks intently into the perfect law of freedom and perseveres in it, and is not a forgetful hearer but one who does good works—this person will be blessed in what he does. If anyone thinks he is religious without controlling his tongue, then his religion is useless and he deceives himself."

How's your juggling?

NOAHism
NOTHING LEFT TO LEARN

"I know my ABCs and all my numbers. I don't think I need to go school!"

DAY 11
BUFFET

When we had kids we started observing how other families structured their schedules in hopes of learning how to be good parents. We didn't have a clue (and we still feel like that at times) what it meant to give our kids an awesome childhood experience, while structuring their lives in a way that brought the desire for godliness and concern for others.

In our observations what we discovered was that parents in our society are very concerned with giving their kids an "American" childhood. So Little Johnny and Suzie are dragged from soccer, to dance, to karate, to church, to play dates, to a babysitter, and on and on. I'm tired after typing that sentence much less being the parent or the child in that scenario.

We decided early to only involve our kids in one activity at a time. They got to choose. If they didn't like it, they would finish the season and move on to the next thing. No dragging our kids all over the countryside in hopes of giving them a true, American childhood.

Not only do we do this with our kids, we do this at church as well. We offer a buffet of choices and make the churchgoer feel less holy if they don't commit to everything. "When I was a kid," we say, "I went to church every time the doors were opened." With this kind of pressure, no wonder people are burning out and falling out of churches rapidly.

What if we simplify things a bit? Let's have a great worship service and carry out every other function of the church through the small groups. How much more impactful would it be if our small groups fellowshipped together, did ministry together, was on mission together, worshipped God and reached the world together? Do you see it? What if we were one in focus because we weren't dragged all over the place by programs? The whole point of a buffet is that they compete against each other, making you get a little of all of it and in the end, making you sick.

Are you tired of the constant "we gotta be everywhere" mentality? Get involved with a small group of people and make it your mission to change your family, change a culture, and change the world with the Gospel of Jesus Christ?

This changes the meaning of Hebrews 10:24-25 a bit in our eyes doesn't it?

"let us be concerned about one another in order to promote love and good works, not staying away from our meetings, as some habitually do, but encouraging each other, and all the more as you see the day drawing near."

NOAHism
LOGICAL SHOPPING

"Momma, if you like it then buy it!"

DAY 12
FOLLOWER

Mark 8:34 says this, "Summoning the crowd along with His disciples, He said to them, 'If anyone wants to be My follower, he must deny himself, take up his cross, and follow me.'" The question that captured my thoughts was, "Who am I following, Jesus or Self?"

The general theme of the day seems to be that we will follow as long as it doesn't disrupt our schedules, relationships, or comfort zones too much. We deny ourselves long enough to put on the facade that we are a fully devoted follower of Jesus Christ, but how do we react when we are asked to give up a day, a week, a month, or a year to fully focus our energies, our time, and our resources for the Kingdom of Christ.?

The disciples struggled with this in Mark 8. They wanted to send the crowd away because they could not see how all of the crowd could be fed. How many times do we walk away or send away the crowd because we can't humanly think how they can be fed spiritually or physically? Jesus is saying, "I have not given you a spirit of fear, but one of power, love, and a sound mind." This power is the Holy Spirit. The power that Jesus used to feed the five thousand.

The foundation for this type of surrender is built through a daily time reading, studying, and meditating on God's Word. Praying to God for the boldness and courage to deny ourself, stand strong in hardships, and to follow Him when we are tired, hungry, and way outside of our comfort zones. This is only the foundation!

My son, Noah, was discouraged the other day because he has a habit of licking his lips and they stay chronically chapped. He said, "I've prayed to God for Him to help me, but He is not!" I explained to him that praying is good and God will answer. God will give him the courage and the right thoughts to stop doing it, but he still has to NOT do it.

The same is true with our surrender. God has given us a spirit of power, love, and a sound mind, but we must still use it. It is like having your dream car sitting in the garage, waxed, gassed up, but it never leaves the garage.

What are you truly surrendering in your service to God?

NOAHism
SECOND LANGUAGE

Nia: I learned how to say "my name is…" today in Spanish. Me llamo Nia.

Noah: Does my name have a me llamo?

DAY 13
SURRENDER

Jesus says in Luke 9:23, "If anyone <u>wants</u> to come with Me, he <u>must</u> deny himself, <u>take</u> up his cross daily, and <u>follow</u> Me."

A few years ago I went through an Adrian Rogers study where he described the difference between commitment and surrender. He said, "When you're committed, you're in control; when you surrender, you relinquish control. If a robber puts a gun to your head, you don't commit your wallet; you surrender it!" (Kingdom Authority by Adrian Rogers)

I am ever amazed at the willingness of American Christians to commit all the way up to the point where they have to surrender something. This one thing could be a character trait or habit, a sinful action, or a freedom for the sake of the better good. We hold on with a death grip!

As I read through the Gospels I see disciples called to

"follow" Jesus. Some were living in sin, but the majority of them where not called out of a destructive lifestyle. They were called out of family businesses and many times there absence meant that their fathers were left with the heavy load of carrying on.

They could have committed, but at the moment of departure, say, "Oh, I can't leave my family. You are really going to require me to leave my family?"

The point is not that all will be called away from their families, but we will be called to sacrifice and surrender, not just commit. What we have to reconcile in our minds is whether the thing we are refusing to surrender if placed on a scale is equal to the call of Christ to "deny himself, take up his cross daily, and follow Me."

I underlined four words above: wants, must, take, and follow. We must exchange the "wants" of this world for the fulfillment of a surrendered life. The "must" is a great imperative to not just commit but to fully surrender. The "take" is a determination to not live an American Christianity lifestyle, but one of a fully surrendered follower of Christ lifestyle. Lastly, the "follow" truly reveals if we are committing on a surface level or surrendering to the core of our being.

When it is your moment, will you just commit or fully surrender?

NOAHism
PROPER EXERCISE

Beth: I need to exercise more.

Noah: You don't need to do that. The only people who need to exercise are really old people who are about to die!

DAY 14
FAITHFUL

What does your week look like? How are your hours being spent? Are you in the midst of a 70 hour work week? Are you scurrying around town taking your kids from activity to activity? Are you in the midst of a conquest of an epic video game or immersed in a TV series marathon?

I firmly believe that nothing is wrong with working hard, keeping your kids active, enjoying video games, or becoming enthralled in a TV series. But what I do believe is if these things are pushing your service to the kingdom into a tight type of schedule or eliminating the time all together, you are way off track and your effectiveness has been erased by the enemy.

As a Christian and a servant of the King, I must always fight the urge to live life as a modern, American Christian. The popular method of "living for Jesus" is a lazy blending of unintentionality and skewed time management and then we wonder why we are not being effective serving our neighbors and friends, why I'm seeing no change in the worldliness of my kids, and why I'm finding no joy serving at church.

When this happens the result is always a projecting outwards. I will try to cover my insecurities by pointing out a perceived injustice from somebody else. My wife is not meeting my needs. The church leadership is not letting me lead. My kids will not follow my leadership.

Luke 16:10 says, "Whoever is faithful in very little is also faithful in much, and whoever is unrighteous in very little is also unrighteous in much." My challenge to you would be to take a step back, take out a sheet of paper, and analyze how you spend your hours. Write down the hours you spend sleeping, eating, watching TV, in ministry, at work, etc. I believe you will quickly see how skewed your life has become and why you are feeling such a sense of insecurity.

I lean firmly on Luke 16:10. Be faithful with your time, your money, your gifts and at the end of the day you can lay your head on your pillow and say, "Today was not wasted. It was a day I lived for the Kingdom."

NOAHism
A PRAYER FOR REGULARITY

"Dear God, please help me poop."

DAY 15
EXCUSES

What excuse are you leaning on today? Do you think you're too young? Too old? Do you feel your past is too bad? Do you feel like you have nothing to offer?

Every time I read Luke 1 and 2, I'm reminded that I have nothing but excuses. I'm either concerned about how much better somebody else is than me at a particular task. Or, I'm worried about how another person views me. Or, countless other excuses that I conjure up from a lack of faith in God.

If you read Luke 1 and 2, you will find an older woman who is barren, a teenager who is a virgin, and a group of people who live "across the tracks," the looked down upon people of the day. All three got to witness a great move of God. And, all three, could have halted and gave tons of excuses about being too young, too old, nobody loves me, or I'm not worth anything.

God looked at all three and did not say, "Why should I

use them?" He looked at all three and say, "Why not?" Elizabeth (older, barren woman) was given the privilege of carrying who would become John the Baptist, the forerunner of Jesus. Mary (teenage virgin) was chosen to carry the Savior of the world. The shepherds (people from across the tracks) were given the privilege of welcoming Jesus into this world in the stable.

The truth of the matter is that what we see as shortcomings, Jesus sees as an opportunity to be glorified. Paul, the greatest missionary and church planter, had a great weakness. Some theologians said it was a sight problem. He asked God to remove it three times. But Jesus told him, "My grace is sufficient for you, for power is perfected in weakness." Paul's conclusion, "I will most boldly boast all the more about my weaknesses, so that Christ's power may reside in me. So I take pleasure in weaknesses, insults, catastrophes, persecutions, and in pressure, because of Christ. For when I am weak, then I am strong." (2 Corinthians 12:9-10)

What excuse do you have? Insults? Catastrophes? Persecutions? Pressure? The choice is: wallow in pity or admit weakness and find strength in Christ.

NOAHism
TWIN TRIPLETS

Peggy: Do you know what triplets are?

Noah: Yes, they are three twins.

DAY 16
CRYING

Luke 3:4, quoting the prophet Isaiah, says, "A voice of one crying out in the wilderness: Prepare the way for the Lord; make His paths straight!"

John the Baptist had one purpose: Prepare the way for the Lord. He was not THE GUY. He was to prepare the way for THE GUY. Even when he got proclaimed to be THE GUY, he stood firm and said, "I am not THE GUY. I am not worthy to untie the strap of His sandals." (loose interpretation of Luke 3)

I'm always amazed when I watch college football or basketball and gaze at the sideline or bench and see multiple coaches. Only THE GUY, the head coach, gets credit for the victory or discredit for the loss, but every one of the coaches are fighting with the team to bring about unity, a single message, and a successful team.

Just like John the Baptist, we each have one purpose: to share a single message - "repentance for the forgiveness of sins (Luke 3:3)." We do this in unity for the glory of God and the furthering of His kingdom.

This will never be fulfilled if we are worried about someone's else's spotlight or position; when we are envious of someone else's success or what some might call "blessings"; when we feel inferior to another's placement in the church. This can only be accomplished when we fulfill our purpose: to live as ambassadors of Christ, sent ones with a message.

"But now God has placed each one of the parts in one body just as He wanted...God has put the body together, giving greater honor to the less honorable, so that there would be no division in the body, but that members would have the same concern for each other. So if one member suffers, all the members suffer with it; if one member is honored, all the members rejoice with it." (1 Corinthians 12:18, 24-26)

The challenge for each one of us is to quit fighting against "the guy" in our church and start fighting for THE GUY who's message we are called to proclaim with unity to bring about success for the team, God's team.

Is your cry one of envy and jealousy or is it one of purpose and team?

NOAHism
FILM RATINGS

"PG-13 means 13 & up can watch the movie. Papa, you can watch every movie because you are very up!"

DAY 17
PURPOSE

I use nearly 100 things in my house for it's purpose before starting my day. I sleep in my bed. I brush my teeth with a toothbrush. I eat cereal with a spoon out of a bowl. I put my shoes on my feet. You get the point. Everything I do to, put in, or put on my body is fulfilling it's purpose and I am directing that purpose.

In Luke 4:43, Jesus says, "I must proclaim the good news about the kingdom of God to the other towns also, because I was sent for this purpose." Jesus fulfilled His purpose. He went from town to town sharing the good news. He left a heritage by way of His disciples to keep doing the same. He had a time of privacy with His Father in Heaven. He is the definition of a balanced, purposeful life.

What about us? Although we use every tool known to man for it's purpose, we seem to forget that our bodies, our hands and feet, our gifts and energies, belong to the Creator of the universe. He designed us specifically for a purpose. I found this purpose for my life (although I have been in the desert and have failed Him mightily many, many times) in 1998, when God directed me to preach. A verse in 1 Corinthians 9:16 clarified this direction, "For necessity is laid upon me, yea, woe is unto me, if I preach not the gospel!"

We all have purpose. We all have gifts. I think deep down most of us realize this, but are stuck in a pattern of conditioning that is called "American Christianity." Go to church, read a few verses, give a little money. Repeat. Minimum requirement met.

1 Corinthians 6:19-20 says, "Don't you know that your body is a sanctuary of the Holy Spirit who is in you, whom you have from God? You are not your own, for you were bought at a price. Therefore glorify God in your body." What if we lived extravagantly surrendered lives for God's glory, the One who bought us with a price, the One who gave us the Holy Spirit, the One who filled us with purpose, the One who showed us how to do this.

Where are you finding purpose today?

NOAHism
EXERCISE REGIMENT

As he was being told to quit wrestling because he would end up crying, Noah says, "But I do 990x (referencing P90x)."

DAY 18
IMMEDIATELY

Have you ever considered how many things in our daily lives that we accept immediately? We set an alarm clock and don't give a second thought to whether it will go off in the morning (whether we want it to or not, that's a different story). We stick our key in the ignition and immediately expect it to start. We sit in various chairs throughout the day without a moment's pause to the possibility of falling to the ground.

Why is it that when we are directed, either by Scripture or leading, to follow Christ in a particular area, situation, or circumstance during the day, that we pause, reflect, meditate, pray, hesitate, and wait for confirmation after confirmation? Pause for a moment and reflect on the magnitude of this contrast. No second thought or pause of things created by man. Much reflection and hesitation to direction from the Creator of the universe. Anybody bothered by this comparison?

We read in Luke 5 where Jesus directs James and John

to quit catching fish and to catch people (v10). The next verse says they "left everything, and followed Him." Immediate reaction to a direction from Jesus. The underside of this story is that their father, Zebedee, is now left to run the family business on his own. This decision put much stress on the family's livelihood. If they would have paused, waited a season, and reflected for a long period of time, they would have missed out on being with Jesus and being a part of launching the first church.

What is God directing you to do? What are you allowing to be a deterrent to being fully used by God? The problem with American Christianity is that we have melted it down to it's minimal usefulness and have called that living "radically" for Christ. We have huddled up and built walls and isolated ourselves from the ministry that we are supposed to be living out.

It is a directive to meditate on God's word, pray, go to church, tithe, and serve the church. But, it is also a directive to live out your faith in practical ways in your family, at work, at school, and be in the world (not of it) impacting a lost culture. My pastor, Stephen Ward, said one Sunday, "We are afraid that if we let our kids have non-Christian friends that they will be a bad influence. They probably will be a bad influence. The bigger question is, are we training our kids to be warriors for Christ who will influence this world?"

Later in Luke 5 four people bring their paralyzed friend to Jesus. Jesus heals the man and tells him to "get up, pick up your mat, and go home (v24)." The next verse says, "Immediately he got up before them, picked up what he had been lying on, and went home glorifying God."

We all have gifts that we are lying around on and squandering. Today, you have permission to "get up, pick up your mat" and go to work for Him. Fulfill your purpose. Use your gifts. Live for Christ.

Later in Luke 5 Jesus directs Levi, a tax collector (cuss word), to follow Him (v27). The next verse says, "So leaving everything behind, he got up and began to follow Him." Ok, same story as before. Listen to what else he did, v29, "Then Levi hosted a grand banquet for Him at his house. Now there was a large crowd of tax collectors and others who were guests with them." He did not isolate himself from the people he had been doing life with. He invited them all to his house to meet the man who changed his life.

The religious leaders scoffed at this notion. Jesus sums up everything with a simple analogy, "The healthy don't need a doctor, but the sick do. I have not come to call the righteous, but sinners to repentance." (v31-32)

We have a huge choice with major implications to make: sit around with the healthy (eating, drinking, and being merry) and talk about how "sick" the world is *or* immediately get up, take up our mats, and invite them to meet the man who changed our lives. If we can immediately react to created objects of man, it is way past time for us to react and respond to the directives of the man who changed everything about us.

NOAHism
MARRIAGE

"Nia, I want you to be my wife so I won't have to have a wedding and do that kissing part."

DAY 19
WRONGED

How has somebody wronged you this week? Did somebody cut you off on the freeway? Cut in line at Wal-Mart? Said hurtful words to you? Or (insert your story here)?

We all know that, if not daily, multiple times during a week, people are going to wrong us. The natural reaction is to overreact. Defriend them on Facebook. Quit talking to them. Or even worse, jump into the mud with them and respond in kind to their hurtful actions.

I'm prone to this like everybody else. Maybe even more so because I am always right. When something of this nature enters my sphere, I naturally push back and think and sometimes respond with how horrible that person is for doing that. They cannot possibly love Jesus with that attitude. Tracking with me?

I love that Jesus doesn't leave us stranded in this sea of agony without a life vest. In Luke 6 Jesus tackles this subject head on:

"But I say to you who listen: Love your enemies, do what is good to those who hate you, bless those who curse you, pray for those who mistreat you. If anyone hits you on the cheek, offer the other also... Just as you want others to do for you, do the same for them. If you love those who love you, what credit is that to you? Even sinners love those who love them. If you do what is good to those who are good to you, what credit is that to you? Even sinners do that... But love you enemies, do what is good, and lend, expecting nothing in return. Then your reward will be great, and you will be sons of the Most High. For He is gracious to the ungrateful and evil. Be merciful, just as your Father also is merciful." (v27-29a, 31-33, 35-36)

Everybody signed up and ready to start living like this? Hard teaching from Jesus. Remember what Jesus said when He was in agony, dying on the cross: "Father, forgive them, for they know not what they do."

Today, we have a choice between overreaction that leads to more stress and more drama and more hurt *or* living out the hard teaching of Jesus and loving our enemies, do good to those who hate us, praying for them, and treating them like we would like to be treated.

Why should we do this? Because it is easy? No, because Jesus did the same for us. Romans 5:8, "But God proves His own love for us in that while we were still sinners (some translations say "enemies"), Christ died for us!"

Be merciful, just as your Father also is merciful!

NOAHism
PE GEOGRAPHY

Sarah: What direction are we going?

Noah: We are going East.

Sarah: Good. How do you know that?

Noah: I take PE.

DAY 20
INHERITANCE

In Luke 10 Jesus sends out 70 disciples, two by two, with a message to share and gives them authority. They return all beside themselves because the spirits listened to them. Jesus takes a moment and then corrects them with "don't rejoice that the spirits submit to you, but rejoice that your names are written in heaven." (Luke 10:20)

Do you see it? Our natural inclination is to get all coo-coo for cocoa puffs because of results or some spiritual success and yearn for appreciation, a pat on the back, some acknowledgement that we are just AWESOME.

Ok, let's flip the coin. The other side of the equation is just as true. When we are rejected, people don't listen to us or accept us, we get down and depressed and think that we are useless and have failed our Savior. Jesus has a word for this in Luke 10:16, "Whoever listens to you listens to Me. Whoever rejects you rejects Me. And whoever rejects Me rejects the One who sent Me."

The truest gauge we can use to determine the right path is to see what Jesus did in these situations. Did Jesus have spiritual successes? Absolutely. Did Jesus deal with rejection? Absolutely. You will find with each side of the coin that Jesus' immediate response was to turn directly to the Father and praise Him, give Him glory, and lean fully in His goodness.

If we are faithful in proclaiming His message and people reject it, they are not rejecting us, they are rejecting Jesus, and in essence, rejecting the One who sent Him, God. If people listen and accept the message, they are accepting Jesus, and in essence, accepting the One who sent Him, God.

The bottom line is found in knowing where our inheritance lies. It is not found in doing good works. It is not affected by rejection. It lies firmly and securely in a relationship with Jesus Christ. Anything and everything that we do stems from this relationship, because of this relationship, not as a continuance of trying to earn our way into this relationship.

Seeing spiritual successes? Praise God. Enduring rejection? Praise God. Your inheritance is secure. Remain faithful!

NOAHism
CHANGING IDENTITY

"When I'm a teenager, I'm changing my name to George."

DAY 21
BLESSED

We bless people when they sneeze. We use it to close a conversation: Have a blessed day! We exclaim it when we are recounting just how good we have it: God is truly blessing us right now! The kids are healthy. We have good jobs. Not only that, God blessed me with the jobs, the clothes, a good school for the kids, a car, and on and on and on.

I'm guilty of this just like you are. We are conditioned as Americans to let loose this phrase as an immediate reaction without any thought to a perceived blessing from God.

Think deeper with me for a moment. Has God blessed us and not the person in the third world with no job, very little clothing, no good school, no car, and on and on and on? Has God blessed us and not the Christian in the Middle East who is suffering from massive persecution for His faith? Has God blessed us and not the person in the United States who's dealing with a terminal illness, loss of job, etc? Has God blessed us and not Jesus and the disciples who suffered great persecution and ultimately death for most of them because of their faith?

You see, what we use so flippantly as a conversation filler is truly not the reality of what being blessed is. Read this passage:

"The poor in spirit are blessed, for the kingdom of heaven is theirs. Those who mourn are blessed, for they will be comforted. The gentle are blessed, for they will inherit the earth. Those who hunger and thirst for righteousness are blessed, for they will be filled. The merciful are blessed, for they will be shown mercy. The pure in heart are blessed, for they will see God. The peacemakers are blessed, for they will be called sons of God. Those who are persecuted for righteousness are blessed, for the kingdom of heaven is theirs. You are blessed when they insult and persecute you and falsely say every kind of evil against you because of Me. Be glad and rejoice, because your reward is great in heaven. For that is how they persecuted the prophets who were before you.
(Matthew 5:3-12 HCSB)

This is a modern translation, but I'm pretty sure that the older translations don't discuss being blessed because of good health, jobs, clothes, schools, cars, and so on. We truly live in a country that is at the pinnacle of success compared to nearly any place on the planet. We are born with a lot of opportunities that a majority of the planet will never see. But blessed, I'm not totally convinced.

To be blessed is to see our weakness and to find strength in God. To be blessed is to find comfort in God when we are hurting. To be blessed is to be meek, moldable, pliable. To be blessed is to yearn and strive after God's goodness with everything that we have. To be blessed is to show mercy to people here and abroad who have not what we have. To be blessed is to strive for holiness. To be blessed is to be at peace with people, not to instigate or join a fight. To be blessed is to be persecuted and insulted for living out the faith of Jesus, who was persecuted for living out the same.

The choice is: to see yourself as a blessed American or to see yourself through the lens of being a blessed Christian and identifying with Jesus and the disciples.

I leave you with a simple command: Have a blessed day!

NOAHism
DENTAL HYGIENE

Nia: Mom, Noah didn't brush his teeth.

Noah: It's Ok. I'll brush my teeth twice tomorrow.

DAY 22
DISCONNECTED

You've probably heard somebody in your lifetime say (or you've said this), "I don't have to go to church to worship God. I can worship Him just fine where I am." God is everywhere. True. You can talk to Him anywhere. True. But this mindset misses the bigger picture.

Jesus was the full embodiment of God. You see this in His character, His service, His humility. On the contrary, we are not the full embodiment of God. We should reflect to the fullest of our abilities His character, His service, and His humility. At the end of the day, we will fall way short (Romans 3:23).

Andy Stanley gives an interesting (and gross) analogy about why we should serve in connection and community with other believers. He tells a FICTIONAL story of a child who gets their hand cut off. The hand is taken and placed in a box. Ten years later, the child grows up, the wound is healed, no hand grows back, but the child grows up. The hand in the box has transformed from a normal hand, to rotting, to dust, and is no longer useful.

We were made to be in connection, in community with one another. The New Testament calls the followers of Christ "the body," we are the church. With Jesus as the head. When we cut ourselves off from the body, we are, over time, allowing ourselves to be transformed from a normal part of the body, to something rotting and gross, and ultimately, to something no longer useful.

Can we have a relationship with Christ without being a part of the church? I think so. Can we having a growing relationship with Christ without the church? No way. We were made to be in connection, in community with one another.

Jesus was the full embodiment of God. We each have been given pieces of His abilities (called gifts) for a purpose: to use them in tandem to fulfill Christ's purpose. Ephesians 4:16 says, "From Him the whole body, fitted and knit together by every supporting ligament, promotes the growth of the body for building up itself in love by the proper working of each individual part."

The next time the thought of being an "island Christian" comes your way think about the impact of this decision. You become gross and no longer useful. You hamper the work of Christ through the body because the church is missing your part (your giftedness).

Is disconnection worth slowing down the work of Christ?

"Nia, I don't have a worship singing voice. I only have a rock n roll voice."

DAY 23
LEFTOVERS

Everyone loves cleaning out the refrigerator, right? Opening plastic container by plastic container. Never knowing what awaits you below each lid. Sometimes it's spaghetti and meatballs. Sometimes it's veggies. And then, sometimes it is just unidentifiable.

I recently had the pleasure of taking in all of the aforementioned aromas and experience the greatness of living in excess. One dish was leftover from New Year's Day (a month earlier). I took a minute in the fog of ruined food and found a moment of clarity, of disgust, and of motivation.

Those little containers of Tupperware are symbols of a bigger problem that plagues us individually, as families, and as a society. We live in our excesses. We rarely give sacrificially and live in necessity.

In Luke 21 Jesus gives an eyewitness account of this very issue:

He looked up and saw the rich dropping their offerings into the temple treasury. He also saw a poor widow dropping in two tiny coins. "I tell you the truth," He said. "This poor widow has put in more than all of them. For all these people have put in gifts **out of their surplus**, but she **out of her poverty has put in all she had** to live on." (v1-4, HCSB)

This is a beautiful picture of where we ultimately place our faith. "The rich" in this account give a lot, but only after living in their excesses. These are the stories that are covered on the news. "Mr. So-and-So gave $100,000 to (fill in the bank) charity. What an amazing act of benevolence!"

"This poor widow" was in direct connection with her God. She wasn't noticed by the religious leaders, the crowd, or the disciples, but Jesus saw her heart. She gave out of what she needed to live on because she had faith that God would provide for her needs. She gave sacrificially and was determined to live in necessity, the necessity of full dependence in God.

I have a friend who is pretty well off, by American standards, but lives in this way. She gives sacrificially to the church, charities, and the needy. She doesn't leave leftovers to waste. She sometimes eats them past the limit of sanity, but you get the point.

Here's the challenge for all of us. The next time you open your refrigerator or eat out and have leftovers from an oversized meal. Think about how you are living. Will this be a moment of clarity? Of disgust? Of motivation? After you and God have determined what you should give, start doing it.

And, eat your leftovers!

NOAHism
NAMING A NEW CHURCH

Noah: Glory to the Highest Bible Church

Nia: Don't Just Sit There Church

DAY 24
ASTONISHMENT

I'm always amazed when I reflect on the events that shock me. There was the time when my students didn't place at our national conference when we had the year before (SHOCK). Another time was when the Cardinals were up on the Braves in the series 3 to 1 and lost the series and the opportunity for the World Series (SHOCK). And the time when my 1984 Ford Ranger locked up about 10 miles from the house (SHOCK).

You've had these shocking moments. What about the unexpected bill that comes in the mail? The unexpected check? When someone was healed? Or unexpectedly died? Or (blank)? We all deal with these moments in life that bring astonishment. Some necessarily so and some come from a lack of focus. Why all the shock?

Acts 3 touches on this subject. The Holy Spirit has just been poured out on the disciples and they are now living out their ministry with the power of the Holy Spirit inside of them. Peter and John are going to temple when they see a beggar who has been crippled for a long time. They tell him in verse 6, "In the name of Jesus Christ the Nazarene, get up and walk!" The people see him walking and praising God so in verse 10 they are "filled with awe and astonishment." And in verse 11, all the people are "greatly amazed."

Let me pause for a minute. Nothing is out of the ordinary at this point. If we saw something like this (and many of us have), we would be "filled with awe and astonishment" as well. Where this story transitions is the section that we miss. Peter and John see what is happening. They change their schedule and focus the attention and amazement in a certain direction. In verse 12, they ask, "why are you amazed at this? Or why do you stare at us, as though we had made him walk by our own power or godliness?"

Do you notice the deflection? Let me be transparent. I probably would hesitate for a moment and bask in the admiration and amazement of the moment. Or give the old, lower my head and say, "It was all God. I'm just an instrument in His hands," speech and show them my JESUS FREAK shirt and wristband.

Peter and John then take it a step forward after the deflection - they turn it to Jesus. They discuss how those who are now amazed were the ones who ushered Jesus into His death through ignorance. They present a conviction moment. From deflection to conviction and then...

Response. Verse 19 says, "Therefore repent and turn back, so that your sins may be wiped out, that seasons of refreshing may come from the presence of the Lord." What a beautiful verse! This is the image of the spring time, when the pollen is heavy and a spring rain washes all that away and refreshes the air and the ground.

We need this refreshing in America. What shocks us should empower us. What leads to awe should lead to inspiration. Think about what it would look like if we followed the pattern of Peter and John:

1. Deflect attention from ourselves.

2. Present a conviction moment by revealing how we are personally responsible.

3. Allow people to respond which, through repentance, will bring about refreshment.

I deflect. The Holy Spirit convicts. People respond. Let's turn our astonishment into action!

NOAHism
IMPORTANCE OF MLK DAY

"I love that he gave us a day off from school."

DAY 25
SOMETHING

We live in a time of great need. We've seen the commercials and know the statistics of how many impoverished people there are on the planet. We've seen the homeless standing on our street corners begging for spare change or spare food. We have seen the economy take a huge toll on our families through loss of jobs, houses, or just a shrinking paycheck and rising costs.

I was recently reminded of how paralyzing it feels to see these massive problems around me and think that I cannot make a dent in solving them. I'm not wealthy (in American terms). I'm very limited in mercy and compassion. And, I am just too busy to help!

In a recent small group lesson a friend of mine, John Wolfe, described a time when he was 12. He had a paper route and as he cut the twine off the papers, 4 or 5 papers flew down the street. He only had just enough papers to complete his route, no extras. Two teenage boys saw what happened and after initially laughing, took a couple minutes and chased down the papers to help him out. Today, 40 years later, those boys probably don't remember that, but John still does. It didn't take much for these boys to make a 40 year impact on John. They were willing to give something to help in a situation where help was needed.

My daughter is a great reminder of this for me as well. She is always so thoughtful of what people are going through. She draws pictures and gives them to people. She gives her stuff away. On Valentine's Day, she divided out her candy, giving a portion of it to her bus driver. She said, "My bus driver has a hard job dealing with teenagers who break the rules everyday. Plus, God placed her as an authority over me." Thoughtfulness is something that, if we slow down, we can give an abundance of to people in our spheres of influence.

In John 6 there's a boy who "has five barley loaves and two fish (v9)." He sees the great need around him as 5,000 men are hungry and he is willing to give something to help in the situation. Unprompted. Not coerced. He willingly offers what he has, which might have meant that he would go hungry in the process. As Paul Harvey would say, the rest of the story ends with Jesus blessing the food, multiplying to feed all in attendance with 12 basketsful of leftovers.

The challenge for all of us is to slow down and remember our purpose for being here. I believe Matthew 5:16 says it well, "let your light shine before men, so that they may see your good works and give glory to your Father in heaven." Shining THE LIGHT takes a connection to the power source to be energized to take the light where it needs to go. Shining THE LIGHT takes a willingness to turn it on when we see darkness. Shining THE LIGHT takes direction to point it where it is needed.

All of us who have a relationship with Jesus Christ have this flashlight of compassion.

What is the something you have? I would challenge you (and me) to take the something (gifts, resources, and energy) to people who need it. You never know what the small act of compassion could mean to somebody 40 years down the road when that moment has long since faded from your memory.

Do something today!

NOAHism
SIBLING INTIMIDATION

"Nia, I'll make you cry in the dark!"

DAY 26
WHY?

I remember a few years ago when my kids were in a very important stage of life, the **WHY** stage. The command from me or Beth could be as simple as throw a piece of paper in the trash and the response from our kids would be, **WHY**. And our response would be, "Because I said so!"

As I've aged I now realize that the **WHY** stage is not a stage after all, it is a reality that we live until we breathe our last. It morphs into more complex issues and sometimes visits the past into the simple, but the fact is that we want to know **WHY**.

Our network of churches constructed resources that are a guide to people as they explore the answer to **WHY**: why do I act the way that I do, why do I have so many challenges, and why do I feel like something is missing.

Matthew 28:18-20 says this,

"Then Jesus came to them and said, "All authority in heaven and on earth has been given to me. Therefore go and make disciples of all nations, baptizing them in the name of the Father and of the Son and of the Holy Spirit, and teaching them to obey everything I have commanded you. And surely I am with you always, to the very end of the age."

Why did my family move across the country to start churches? Because Jesus said GO and MAKE DISCIPLES. Obedience makes us answer the question of **WHY** in ways that are countercultural. The answer most of the time is contrary to the American Dream and will be viewed, by religious people and people in the world, as very odd.

So why did we do what we did? Because JESUS said so...

NOAHism
CULTURAL FASHION

"Look Daddy, I'm wearing socks and flip flops. If they can do it Japan, I can do it here."

DAY 27
IMPACT

I loved college and being the good steward that I was I stretched my four year degree into seven years and incurred a lot of debt in the mean time. I entered college with three scholarships and financial aid. I was being paid to go to college because of graduating as an honor graduate. After one semester, I had lost all of my scholarships and had to get a job.

Later into my decade of college, I had to get school loans. And, I also signed up for a credit card to put emergency things on like meals at nice restaurants and name-brand clothes and Christmas gifts for family and friends.

At the same time this all was going on, Beth graduated high school as her class valedictorian, got a full scholarship with room and board to college, kept it, graduated #2 in her college class, all while not working and incurring no debt.

We got married after college and she got the great privilege of helping pay off all the debt I brought into the marriage. My decade of stupidity led to the ripple effect of another decade of paying all of that off.

1 Timothy 6:17-19 says this, "Instruct those who are rich in the present age not to be arrogant or to set their hope on the uncertainty of wealth, but on God, who richly provides us with all things to enjoy. Instruct them to do what is good, to be rich in good works, to be generous, willing to share, storing up for themselves a good reserve for the age to come, so that they may take hold of life that is real."

We are not owners of anything; we are stewards. The finances that have been entrusted to us are by the goodness of God. Having these finances ought to humble us and cause us to want to make an impact for God, not for ourselves.

It is our responsibility and our happiness is found in using all that we have for God and in impacting others. Just like Jesus modeled when He gave up all of His riches and became poor for our sakes.

We should use our finances to do good for others; we should share; we should put our money to work. When we do, we build ourselves up spiritually, and we make investments for the future

Adrian Rogers, one of my favorite preachers, says, "When you die, you are going to leave behind all that you have, and you are going to take with you all that you are."

What impact are you making with what's been entrusted to you?

NOAHism
BEDTIME

Me: I'm ready for bed.

Noah: I'm ready for bed when my body tells me it's time.

DAY 28
CONNECT

Before my family and I moved to Washington, I taught Jr. High Computer Technology for 10 years. From my first year of teaching till now, the advances in technology have been amazing.

There's a great, old commercial that demonstrates this rapid growth. It shows someone driving down the road, seeing a billboard with the newest computer so he goes to the store and buys it. When he's heading home, on the same billboard, he sees a worker changing the sign to an even newer computer.

These new technologies have brought the world within reach from your keyboard. We are more connected to each other than at any time in history, but, at the same time, we are becoming more distant in our relationships because of the surface-level Facebook posts and the 140 character Tweets.

We are losing touch with some valuable social skills as

we dive further into technology. Why go have a coffee with someone when you can FaceTime; why call someone when I can text; why get together with my friends when we can electronically connect through our gaming system?

Hebrews 10:23-25 says, "Let us hold on to the confession of our hope without wavering, for He who promised is faithful. And let us be concerned about one another in order to promote love and good works, not staying away from our worship meetings, as some habitually do, but encouraging each other, and all the more as you see the day drawing near."

These three verses lay out a very important progression. V23 starts with us needing to "hold on to the confession of our hope without wavering." The confession of our hope is a relationship with Jesus Christ. We can try to put our hope in lots of different things, but none of them are faithful like He is.

Every football season I have great hope that this is going to be the year that the Browns win more than 5 games in a season and make the playoffs. In 2013 they were actually in first place through five weeks before destroying my hope, finishing the season losing 10 of 11 games.

That's a drastic example of hope, but think about your life. Where are you placing your hope? Relationships? Career? Possessions? Health? All of these have a definite beginning and ending point. A relationship with Jesus Christ is eternal and affects our treatment of our relationships, career, possessions, and health.

It starts with a relationship with Jesus Christ, then, continues to v24 and 25, a true concern for others, where we have to create an atmosphere that promotes love and good works and encouragement. A relationship with God should not remain internal and personal; it must spread to others. Notice, that a personal hope in Jesus, overflows into a gathering of people where you are not concerned with your own needs, but the needs of others. Concern for them, love for them, good works for them, encouragement for them.

Are you truly connecting with people in a way that takes more than 140 characters?

NOAHism
REWRITING BIBLE STORIES

Me: What had happened in David's past that made him trust God would be with him?

Noah: He helped him kill a lion.

Nia: And a bear.

Noah: And I think there was also a cheetah!

DAY 29
PASSION

The channels are filled with "passionate" people hopping from bed to bed because "you can't help whom you love." Or, we see stadiums filled with painted up, screaming, passionate fans cheering on their favorite team. Or, in shows like Survivor or The Amazing Race, we see people stretch themselves to the brink of death through sheer passion and determination to reach the finish line as the winner.

Probably the most difficult thing along these lines that I have ever done that required this type of passion is to run a marathon. I trained for months before the race day. Getting up early on Saturdays to put in 10, 15, 20 miles. I would run 3 or 4 other days during the week, either early in the morning or in the afternoon. I had to watch what I ate the day before because it would revisit me in my run.

Finally, after all of this preparation, race day was here. I took off, watching my pace, staying hydrated. I got to the halfway point and I was 20 minutes ahead of pace.

What a feeling! I was cruising along happy with how I was feeling.

Then, at mile 18, my left calf froze up. No panic. I went over to the curb stretched it out for a few seconds. I was still ahead of pace. No worries. I took off again. ½ of a mile later, my right calf froze up. I repeated what I had done before and took off again. A little worry started to set in. My cushion of time was evaporating!

At mile 19, both legs froze up and I knew I was in trouble. The last 7.2 miles were a nightmare. I could only run in short bursts and then stretch out. I was now behind pace. Then, at mile 23 or so, my goal time passed me by. The emotional drain of the day took it's toll! I finished the race about 15 minutes above my goal, very upset.

Thinking back to my prep time for the marathon, I had started on track, very good schedule that I stuck to, but in the final month before the race, I started skipping some days. A long run here and a speed day there and this revealed itself at mile 18 when I hit a wall that I couldn't fight through solely on passion.

True godly passion is driven by selflessness, a desire for preparing ourselves in a way that doesn't follow our hearts into various directions, but in a way that will lead our hearts in a direction for love of our God and love for the people around us to see us all become passionate in our pursuit of Christ.

Colossians 3:12-14 says, "Therefore, God's chosen ones, holy and loved, put on heartfelt compassion, kindness, humility, gentleness, and patience, accepting one another and forgiving one another if anyone has a complaint against another. Just as the Lord has forgiven you, so you must also forgive. Above all, put on love —

the perfect bond of unity. "

When we are truly passionate about something, it drives us outside of our comfort zones and selfishness and then we do something about it. This is where v13 comes in, how we can truly "accept others" and "forgive others." In my interactions with people this week, was I able to put on heartfelt compassion, kindness, humility, gentleness, and patience so that the result would be accepting others and forgiving others just as I have been forgiven?

Continue supporting your favorite teams with passion and emotion. Continue setting goals and reaching them by your drive and passion. But Serve God with passion that is driven by eternity and thankfulness to God, not by the temporary and selfish desires.

BIRTHPLACE GERMS

Nia: Can I have a drink of your Gatorade?

Noah: No way! I'm not getting your germs.

Nia: We are in the same family so you will not get any germs.

Noah: We might be in the same family, but we are from different countries.

DAY 30
PARTNERSHIP

I remember when Beth and I were in college we were asked to do a reading at church together. I signed up with her. We practiced our lines together for a few weeks. Then, the night of the event happened. All the people of the church showed up. Beth showed up. But I did not. I came later after my lines. What an idiot! If I didn't know it before I saw Beth's face, I definitely knew it once I saw her glare from across the room.

Unfortunately, I could share countless, idiotic stories of me not showing up in our relationship and for our relationship. We all have been that person or we are glaring at that person right now. Emotions only carry us so far. We have to actually show up and do the work whether it is something fun we are experiencing as a couple or it is something difficult.

In Genesis, all the animals were paraded in front of Adam for him to name and no "compliment," no "helper" was found there. God puts Adam into a deep sleep and takes a rib, and creates woman, Eve, the mother of all living. Adam awakens to this creature that makes his heart swell and dance in his chest. She is the completion of what he is missing. He notices the beautiful radiance of her image, the perfect image of God.

As Adam saw Eve for the first time, I remember seeing Beth for the first time and I was immediately captivated by her. Then, on our wedding day, I felt the same way. The "for better" was really good and we were invincible and could experience anything.

How we deal with what comes next after those amazing memories is what shapes our relationships to thrive during the for worse times or to wither into bitterness and brokenness.

I often hear people bash Eve for taking the fruit and Adam for not doing what God commanded him to do. What I do not hear a lot about is the longevity of Adam and Eve's marriage. Get this picture. They went from a perfect state of heavenly unity with God to our stark reality, fallen humanity in a split-second.

Today's divorce rate is around 50%, whether it is a couple inside the church or outside of the church. In Adam and Eve's time there was not a divorce rate and they did not begin the "trend." This God created, hard-working couple is a shimmering example of longevity through the "for worse" times.

Today's couples, flippantly break marriage covenants like they break cell-phone contracts. They are all about the "for better," but they swiftly scuttle away from the "for worse."

Remember, the consequence of Adam & Eve's disobedience is painful toil in their work & childbirth, but marriage in itself takes painful toil at times to thrive. But to be able to fully complement each other and to thrive through better or worse, we must do everything just as Colossians 3:23 says, "Whatever you do, do it enthusiastically, as something done for the Lord and not for men."

Jesus, in the greatest "for worse" moment in history took the brutal beating of man, the hanging of Himself on the cross as a criminal, the mocking of the crowd, all with strength harnessed and a wholehearted love for you me so that we would have the opportunity to experience the greatest "for better" time through a relationship with Him and then to live out a picture of the relationship of the church and Jesus in our marriage relationships through fully complimenting each other.

Is your partnership more of a 50/50 contract or a 100/100 covenant of thriving in the "for better" or "for worse" moments of life?

NOAHism
DEPARTMENT STORE &
CHRISTIAN ARTIST MASHUP

Noah: Can we go to TobyMac and get a present for Kaiden?

Beth: You mean TJ Maxx, right?

DAY 31
KNOWING

When I think of bold prayers, I think of those people who are "prayer warriors." You probably know a few of these people or you may be one yourself. They battle daily not for themselves, but for those they come in contact with on a daily basis. They are like the great gladiators of the day who go to combat with their heartfelt words to God and see significant things happen because of that. They have these big prayer journals that, if they wanted to boast, but they don't, they could show you months & months of prayer requests and exactly how God answered those prayers.

Now, I know I'm not the only one, but this seems overwhelming for me. I've tried to keep a prayer journal on many occasions and just can't keep it up. There may be many of you who have run into this same wall. You have the desire, you have the faith, you have the want to. But, you feel like you DON'T KNOW ENOUGH or you DON'T KNOW THE RIGHT WORDS TO SAY or you don't know whether to pray for relief or boldness to weather a storm?

I'm probably pretty similar to you that most of the time I'm just overthinking what I'm supposed to do when I talk to God through prayer. I'm comparing myself to those "warriors" of prayer and losing the focus of what my connection with God should look like. Bold prayers come from WHO you know, not WHAT you know.

Isn't that so true? It's about the relationship. There's not a whole lot of difference in our communication with God, as there is with a loved one. Your significant other or best friend, at the end of the day, is not so much concerned about the hours of time you spend STUDYING them or the long essays you might write about their importance to you as they are with how you communicate with them, how you share your heart, share your concerns, let them in to a place where you harbor the hurts, weaknesses, failings.

In Acts 4, we see this played out through two of the closest disciples of Jesus, Peter and John, talking to some of their closest friends, and then them collectively having a conversation with God. This comes right on the heels of Peter and John being arrested for preaching about Jesus' resurrection and seeing over 5,000 men start a relationship with Jesus.

Can you imagine the shockwaves that went through the religious society of the day? These are 5,000 people who have decided to follow Jesus in the infancy of the church! So, the Jewish leaders of the day arrest Peter & John, interrogate them, and they continue to proclaim Jesus as being the only place where salvation is found. In v13 their boldness is seen, not by what they know, it says they were "uneducated men," but by who they know, they had "been with Jesus."

As the Executive Pastor of our network of churches,

Pinnacle & The Edge right now, with many to come in the future, there are many things that I can't just "strategize" or think my way through because I have a title and I have a Master's degree in Bible & Theology. At the end of the day, those things mean very little if I'm not daily communicating with God. Boldly coming to Him and outlining the issues, praying for boldness to proclaim the message of salvation, and asking for His intervention.

Life is not about being free from problems. It's not about being overwhelmed and overcome by your problems or finding a quick fix to your problems. It's about boldly praying to God, having an honest conversation, and getting up BOLDLY proclaiming His message in spite of your issues and circumstances.

Can you imagine what life would be like if we lived like this? Where our first step is to talk to God, not post, tweet, text, gossip, pop a pill, drown in drink, get in a fight, strategize, live in self-sufficiency?

When we're dealing with a disease, a loss of a job, hurt from a fellow-Christian, persecution, or are just running into a wall that we can't get around, that we can come to a group of people, report everything, raise our voices together to God, and walk out renewed for the battle that will face us.

Bold prayers come from who you know, not what you know.

NOAHism
WIT OVER ATTENTIVENESS

Noah: I'm building a house in the dirt.

Baseball Coach: Pay attention to the batter so he doesn't break your windows out.

Noah: It's Ok. My windows are up!

DAY 32
HOLDING ON

Meal planning is so complex. My wife and I usually plan out 2 weeks in advance. It's like a business strategy meeting. We have a calendar outlining the events of the next two weeks, so we will know when we must cook quick meals, eat out, or when we actually will have time to cook a good meal. We have our budget file open on the computer so we know what we can *or* more truthfully, what we cannot buy. We have to think about meals that don't cause me much acid reflux and meals that possibly will get our kids to eat some sort of vegetable.

There are times, though, when I feel shallow, when I pout about having to put groceries back on the shelf in the store because we have reached zero in our budget when 100's of millions of people in the world will never get an opportunity to have food stored up for two weeks.

The deeper I get in my faith with God, the more uncomfortable I become with being comfortable in my little world while the lives of billions on this planet are crumbling. Call me cynical or call me radical, but

American Christianity is not Biblical Christianity. We hold firmly to the temporary things of life and almost let go of what has eternal value.

Matthew 5:31-32 says, "So don't worry, saying, 'What will we eat?' or 'What will we drink?' or 'What will we wear?' For the idolaters eagerly seek all these things, and your heavenly Father knows that you need them." Jesus is not saying don't prepare meal plans. He's asking, "What captures your time and energy?" "What is your priority?"

V33 continues, "But seek first the kingdom of God and His righteousness, and all these things will be provided for you." What am I holding too tightly? What might Christ call me to let go of?

To truly be disciples, we need to discover the areas in our lives that are idolatrous. What do we hold so tightly that we cannot possibly have a grip on being a disciple?

If I was truly honest and stopped and assessed my life, I reflect very little on Christ. I think I could quickly be pinpointed as an American with shallow interests. I love my world too much to leave my world in an all out sprint after God's interests.

To be a disciple means to follow Jesus, unconditionally, putting our lives completely in His hands. When we say that we want to be His disciple, and then say as the man in Luke 9 says, "I will follow You, Lord, but," we are showing ourselves to be too concerned with our world and thus, not willing to deny ourselves and take up our crosses and follow Jesus.

There comes a time in all of our Christian lives that we must stop the game of American Christianity. Truly assess what we have been holding on to with an iron clad grip, shifting our main focus to being a disciple of Christ.

Jesus is simply saying, "Follow Me. If anyone wants to come with Me, he must deny himself, take up his cross daily, and follow Me. For whoever wants to save his life will lose it, but whoever loses his life because of Me will save it. What has a man benefited if he gains the whole world, yet loses his soul?"

NIAism
VETTING SOURCES

Nia: Did you know that bacon comes from a pig's bottom?

Beth: Really? How did you find that out?

Nia: I know it's true because a 4th grader told me.

DAY 33
MIRROR

Proverbs 27:19 says, "As the water reflects the face, so the heart reflects the person." The reflection a mirror gives has always made me think deeply. I like to stand in front of the mirror and just gaze. My wife can testify to that. She's caught me on several occasions. She would say that I was looking at how good I look (or not look). I don't know what I'm looking for, but one fact is always found in the reflection: my face reflects my face.

Do you remember the cartoon of the ugly duckling? Everything was good with the duck. He tried to play with the other ducks. He swam along with the rest. They had all their ducks in a row. He tried to quack like them. Then came the moment of truth. He saw himself in the water. His face reflected his face. Absolute truth hit him square in the beak. He eventually found his place and lived happily-ever-after.

We play the part of the ugly duckling when we are outside of God's desired purpose for our lives. We are the duck when we are being seen with the wrong crowd. It is our role when we care more about how we look to the world than how God sees us. Most people in this situation do not realize it until they slow down and peer into the mirror that reflects their face, God's mirror.

Our priorities show who we are. Jesus said in Matthew 6:21, "For where your treasure is, there your heart will be also." Our priorities mold our living.

I am truly convinced that we are not a depraved people mainly because we commit open, visible, wild sins, but because we sin just the same by spending our time on useless things and omitting the things that deepen our faith.

- We must choose to study God's Word regularly.
- We must choose to pray regularly.
- We must choose to attend church regularly.
- We must choose to forgive when we are wronged and ask for forgiveness when do wrong.

Getting involved in the things of God must be a priority. Charles Spurgeon says, "A man must know the Lord by the life of real faith, or he can have no true rejoicing in the Lord's worship, his house, his Son, or his ways. Dear reader, how fares it with thy soul?"

What do you see when you look in the mirror?

NIAism
THE PERFECT DATE

Nia: I don't think amusement parks make good date places.

Beth: Why is that?

Nia: Because there's too many thrills and excitement and not enough romance.

DAY 34
ILLNESS

The church is in trouble. I know what you're thinking: "I know it. The world has taken away prayer in schools, the Ten Commandments from public places, abortion is legal, Christians have no rights these days." That's not why the church is in trouble.

All of these are symptoms of the illness. The church is not consumed in doing God's will. The church is not consuming spiritual food. The church does not have a consuming fire for the lost. Christians don't want to give up their idols. Christians don't want to give the church and Sunday back to the Lord. Christians don't want to give themselves to God's Word.

This is the illness. And it has spread like the plague all over our country. That's why other countries are sending many missionaries to the United States. America is not blessing God.

What are you willing to do as an individual to help the church as a whole get back on track?

NOAHism
INVISIBILITY

Me: How was your school day?

Noah: Guess what? My teacher didn't even know I was there. She didn't ask me one thing.

DAY 35
CONSUMED

At a Men's Breakfast at our former church I asked this question: Is the church today a picture of what Jesus imagined? At times, this question consumes my mind as I think about what we, as the church, are doing to impact this world. The answer at the breakfast was a unanimous "no". And I'm sure today it would the same.

So, it brings to mind a second question: why are we continuing the way we are and not striving to be the church that Jesus pictured? I believe the answer is that our comfort has become more important than our convictions.

There needs to be some changes.

First of all, the church should be consumed in doing God's will. Matthew 15:8 says, "These people draw near to Me with their mouth, and honor Me with their lips, but their heart is far from Me. And in vain they worship Me." We've got to get back to the heart of worship. It's all about Jesus.

Secondly, the church should be consuming spiritual food. Folks, the lack of growth of the church numerically is mirrored by the lack of growth of God's people. If we are not growing individually, we will not grow as a church.

Last but not least, the church should have a consuming fire for the lost. This is the Great Commission. Matthew 28:19-20, "Go therefore and make disciples of all the nations, baptizing them in the name of the Father and of the Son and of the Holy Spirit, teaching them to observe all things that I have commanded you…"

Is your church the church Jesus pictured? What part do you play in helping the church be the picture that Jesus had in mind?

NOAHism
NEW CLOTHES

Beth: Daddy got you some
new clothes today.

Noah: Oh man. That just
means I have more laundry to
fold.

DAY 36
BEWARE

God gives me inspiration and guidance from lots of different areas. He's given me dreams where He's laid out a message for me. He's helped me to focus in on bumper stickers, radio advertisements, comments from people, and of course, Scripture.

Awhile back, I was skimming the paper when a headline jumped out at me, "Beware the Salt of the Earth." Now, being the spiritual giant that I am, I instantly thought of Matthew 5:13, "You are the salt of the earth. But if the salt should lose its taste, how can it be made salty? It's no longer good for anything but to be thrown out and trampled on by men."

So, I was left to think about, why should I beware of the salt of the earth?

Imagine for a moment that I am holding two salt shakers. How do we know they are salt shakers? We know they are salt shakers because we have experience looking at salt shakers. We know this is what they look like. The outside of the two salt shakers is the same. They are both glass. They both have silver lids with holes so that the salt can come out. But beware these two salt shakers are very different. One contains salt. The other contains sugar.

This is why we have to beware the salt of the earth. Because the salt of the earth may be really sugar. What we would call the radically changed may just be the radically churched.

As 2 Timothy 3:5 says, the radically churched "have a form of godliness but deny its power." Beware the salt of the earth, they may really be sugar. You can be radically changed from being radically churched with one decision. Romans 10:13 says, "For everyone who calls on the name of the Lord will be saved."

Acts 4:12-13 continues this sentiment, "There is salvation in no one else, for there is no other name under heaven given to people, and we must be saved by it." When they observed the boldness of Peter and John and realized that they were uneducated and untrained men, they were amazed and recognized that they had been with Jesus."

Are you the salt of the earth or are you too busy trying to be sugar to the world?

NOAHism
MISUNDERSTOOD COMPLIMENT

While playing Super Mario
Bros.,

Noah: Nia, you are so pretty!

Nia: (confused look)

Noah: Not in real life. Your
guy on the game!

Nia: (relieved smile)

DAY 37
WALKING

Enoch and Noah are bound together by one phrase in Genesis 5 and 6, they "walked with God." They are the only two men in Scripture who have this said of them. This is the reason we named our son Noah. We prayed before he was born and we still pray this today, that Noah will walk with God.

There are only 4 verses in the entire Bible that say anything about how Enoch lived his life, which, at first glance, seems unusual for a man who was placed in a special category, that he "walked with God" and "never saw death," and don't forget that Methuselah was his son who is oldest person who has ever lived, who died at the young age of 969.

Enoch walked with God. He walked with God because he saw two little eyes staring up at him and he knew that that little boy deserved the best and he knew that the best was found in a relationship with God.

Now, I'm telling you the same, whether you are a

parent or not, there is no bigger decision that can make a bigger impact on your life than the decision to truly follow Christ. People like to stress all the stuff you have to give up to become a Christian.

Let me stress all the stuff you gain from becoming a Christian: love, joy, peace, an eternity in heaven, a relationship with God, and a family of believers to hold you up when the road is long and curvy. Don't put off that decision any longer. Walk with God by following Christ.

NOAHism
AGING

Noah: Why is your skin wrinkled?

Beth: Because my skin is 34 years old.

Noah: I thought it was 54 years old!

DAY 38
ANOINTED

What we know about Lucifer is that he was anointed, blameless, beautiful, wise, and powerful. What a creation of God! But he could not handle the greatness that he was created in to. He became proud and forsook his splendor for corruption. What have people said about you that made you take your gaze from God onto self? Have you ever felt a little "puffed up"? Exalted?

I have been there. At the ripe age of 26 I pastored my first church. I heard the words of "anointed" and "wisdom". How greatly I failed! Sixteen months later my family and I, battered and bruised, were headed back north in a moving truck to Arkansas. My failure came from self-sufficiency. I had a great plan. I had tough skin. I had study habits to deliver a great message. What I did not have was a quiet time...or a prayer life...or life choices that lived up to "anointed and "wise". I soared on Sunday morning, but crash-landed on Monday.

We need to keep ourselves focused on the following facts. First, Lucifer was created in great magnificence, but he let pride cause him to fall "like a lightning flash."

Second, any authority that we now currently possess is deeply rooted in Jesus Christ. In John 15:5 Jesus says, "I am the vine; you are the branches. The one who remains in Me and I in him produces much fruit, because you can do nothing without Me."

Third, our ultimate joy is not in self or how many people are patting us on the back, but in the fact that we have a relationship with Jesus Christ. Our joy is then multiplied when we are "sent out" to share the message of hope and we play a part in other people starting that same relationship.

NOAHism
TECHNOLOGY OVERLOAD

"Can we text Mr. Brian on the iPad so we can play his Wii?"

DAY 39
PRIORITIZING

2 Timothy 3:16-17 says this, "All Scripture is inspired by God and is profitable for teaching, for rebuking, for correcting, for training in righteousness, so that the man of God may be complete, equipped for every good work.

I don't think many people would disagree that how we spend our time reveals what our priorities are and what's most important to us.

My kids have very different priorities. Nia loves to read. Almost everywhere I go in the house she has a book. She unzips her backpack and books fall out all over the place. She is also very relational. She loves people. She'll lay down her book in a heartbeat if the neighbor girls are outside. She plays video games and does other things, but they are way down the priority list.

Noah loves video games. We have to set very strict guidelines on his time playing or we would never see him. When he earns rewards for good behavior, he wants to buy APPs or upgrade existing APPs. If the neighbor kids are outside, he doesn't even notice. He does have friends in the neighborhood and does go to their houses, but what does he want to do when he's there, he wants to plays video games.

Our priorities will drive what we are spending our time doing. Is personal study a priority to you? What about sitting under Bible teaching at a church? Are you a part of a small group? Do you talk about Scripture with others?

All four of these questions reveal our priorities as it comes to the use of Scripture. When we properly prioritize these in our lives, they will enable us to carry out v17, "so that the man of God may be complete, equipped for every good work."

You can own every translation of Bible. You can know where all of the churches and small groups are. You can think about talking to others about faith. But, these things are only as good as you make them a priority in your life.

Just like buying exercise equipment or joining a gym doesn't help unless you use the equipment or go to the gym. You can't will it to be so and it is.

I can try and you can try to will that our faith will grow, but it only happens by practically prioritizing how we are going to learn and apply Scripture to our lives.

BETH-liner
FAMILIAR SAYINGS

"Now, that's the camel that broke the straw's back."

DAY 40
FEAR

I have faced my share of fears. Fear of heights. Fear of girls. Fear of public speaking. I have overcome many of my fears through maturity and through my faith, but one fear still firmly remains: the fear of death.

In 2001 I sat on my parent's couch watching in surreal reality the final breaths of my mom. She was only 51. Her dad had died in his thirties. Her sister had died in her forties. Her brother in his fifties. I continue to have a fear of premature death. What would my family do if they lost me? What would I do if I lost them? Would I be a man quoted as having "perfect integrity"?

The writer of Job sets the stage with a single character standing stage center with a spotlight revealing the strong character of Job. "He was a man of perfect integrity who feared God and turned away from evil (Job 1:1b)." The story of Job is widely cited as a man who was able to persevere through immense suffering. The man who lost everything: servants, possessions, livelihood, family, and health. The man who retained everything: integrity,

Godly reverence, and resistance of evil.

Job is described four times in the book that bears his name as having reverential fear of God. More times than the four Gospels combined. More times than any one book in the New Testament. More times than is said about any other person mentioned in the Bible.

Having a real fear of the Lord should give me the desire every morning to wake up, stroll through my house, look at my wife, my kids, my life, nature and fall on my face and worship God that He is in control of everything. Proverbs 1:7 says, "The fear of the Lord is the beginning of knowledge."

I firmly believe that "fear of the Lord" should be a deepening process that mirrors diving into the ocean. At first, you see very little, but as you dive deeper you see the richness of spiritual life, the diversity of exploring a very real, alive relationship with the creator of life. You experience the fullness of abundant life.

Psalm 128:1-4 shares this song, "How happy is everyone who fears the Lord, who walks in His ways! You will surely eat what your hands have worked for. You will be happy, and it will go well for you. You wife will be like a fruitful vine within your house, your sons, like young olive trees around your table. In this very way the man who fears the Lord will be blessed."

FAMILIAR SAYINGS

"It's nothing to write a letter about."

DAY 41 AND BEYOND
CONTINUE

The ever-famous "they" say it takes forty days to create a habit. You have reached forty-one. What now?

My prayer is that you will continue exploring a deeper faith by daily studying, thinking about, and applying God's Word to your life.

If it has been awhile or you have never systematically read the Bible, I would challenge you to start in the book of John (it's the fourth book of the New Testament). This book will strengthen the foundation you have in Christ, but also challenge you to take greater steps of faith.

As you are doing this, to make this time impactful, ask yourself the following questions and write down the answers.

1. What does the passage say?
2. What do I need to obey?
3. What do I need to relay?
4. How do I need to pray?

These questions will help you to keep what you're reading in context, to apply what you're learning, share with others, and talk to God about your new insights and what you're struggling with.

Stay strong, continue on, and pass it on.

ABOUT THE AUTHOR

Brad Guest is the Executive & Small Groups Pastor for the Pinnacle Church Planting Network in Spokane, Washington. He has served churches in Louisiana and Arkansas.

He also wrote *Surviving the Spiritual War,* which takes a look at Lucifer, creation, Job, and the teachings of Jesus to bring to light the reality of warfare and to give you some tools for battling through the warfare you will encounter.

He has a desire to provide a practical discussion of Biblical issues, to help people fulfill their calling as disciples of Jesus Christ.

Made in the USA
San Bernardino, CA
28 April 2014